DOMINOES

T0040088

Mulan

STARTER LEVEL   250 HEADWORDS

OXFORD
UNIVERSITY PRESS

Great Clarendon Street, Oxford OX2 6DP

Oxford University Press is a department of the University of Oxford.
It furthers the University's objective of excellence in research, scholarship,
and education by publishing worldwide in

Oxford New York

Auckland Cape Town Dar es Salaam Hong Kong Karachi
Kuala Lumpur Madrid Melbourne Mexico City Nairobi
New Delhi Shanghai Taipei Toronto

With offices in

Argentina Austria Brazil Chile Czech Republic France Greece
Guatemala Hungary Italy Japan Poland Portugal Singapore
South Korea Switzerland Thailand Turkey Ukraine Vietnam

OXFORD and OXFORD ENGLISH are registered trade marks of
Oxford University Press in the UK and in certain other countries

ISBN: 978 0 19 424706 1 BOOK
ISBN: 978 0 19 463917 0 BOOK AND AUDIO PACK

No unauthorized photocopying

Printed in China

This book is printed on paper on certified and well-managed sources.

ACKNOWLEDGEMENTS

Illustrations by: Kanako Damerum and Yuzuru Takasaki.

The publisher would like to thank the following for permission to reproduce photographs: Alamy Stock
Photo pp41 (Tokyo Disneyland/Anirban Basu), 41 (Woman wearing kimono/Jean-Philippe
Soule/Around the World in a Viewfinder); Bridgeman Images pp40 (Vase with Painted
Floral Scrolls, Chinese School, Ming Dynasty/Indianapolis Museum of Art, USA/Gift of Mr
and Mrs Eli Lilly & J.W. Alsdorf), 41 (Ivory okimono of people playing Go by Sei, Japanese,
19th century/Private Collection); Shutterstock p18 (Nine Ring Broad sword/Darren
Pullman); Corbis p40 (Yangtze River/Liu Liqun); Mary Evans Picture Library p13 (Woman
weaving using loom, China); OUP pp40 (Great Wall of China/Photodisc), 40 (The Forbidden
City/Photodisc), 40 (Chinese dumplings/Sylvain Grandadam), 41 (Mt. Fuji/Photodisc), 41
(Japanese Bullet Train/Digital Vision), 41 (sushi/Maksim Toome).

DOMINOES

Series Editors: Bill Bowler and Sue Parminter

Mulan

Retold by Janet Hardy-Gould

Illustrated by Kanako Damerum
and Yuzuru Takasaki

Janet Hardy-Gould has worked as a teacher of English for many years. In her free time she enjoys reading history books and modern novels, visiting other European countries, and drinking tea with her friends. She lives in the ancient town of Lewes in the south of England with her husband, and their two children. She has written a number of books, including *Henry VIII and his Six Wives*, and *King Arthur* in the Oxford Bookworms series, and *The Great Fire of London*, *Sinbad* and *Ibn Battuta* in the Dominoes series.

OXFORD
UNIVERSITY PRESS

BEFORE READING

1 Look at these things. Who does them more often? Write *Men* or *Women*.

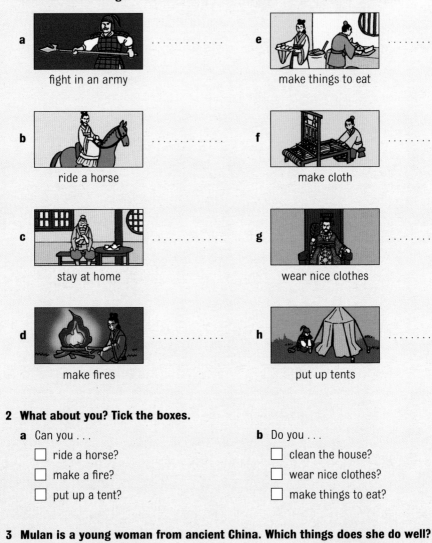

a . . . .
fight in an army

e . . . .
make things to eat

b . . . .
ride a horse

f . . . .
make cloth

c . . . .
stay at home

g . . . .
wear nice clothes

d . . . .
make fires

h . . . .
put up tents

2 What about you? Tick the boxes.

  a Can you . . .

    ☐ ride a horse?

    ☐ make a fire?

    ☐ put up a tent?

  b Do you . . .

    ☐ clean the house?

    ☐ wear nice clothes?

    ☐ make things to eat?

3 Mulan is a young woman from ancient China. Which things does she do well?

She wears nice clothes.

. . . .

. . . .

. . . .

Mulan

CHAPTER 1

Our story begins with a young girl in **ancient** China.

Her name is Hua Mulan.

She lives with her **parents**, her older sister, and her younger brother in a little village.

ncient very old   **parent** a mother or a father

One morning, Mulan is working in her room.
She is making **cloth** to **sell** at the **market**.

Suddenly, she hears a noise.
She goes to the window and
looks out. A lot of people are
running down the street.

Mulan sees her friend, Sun Ying.
'What's the matter?' asks Mulan.
'Quick! Come and see,' says Sun Ying.

cloth you make clothes from this   **sell** to take money for something   **market** where people go to sell things in the street

Mulan **follows** Sun Ying through the village. 'Wait for me!' **shouts** Mulan.

They soon see a big **crowd** of people in front of them.

Everybody is looking at a long **list** on a tree. 'Move! I can't see!' says an old woman at the back. 'Stop that!' shouts a man at the front angrily.

follow to go after someone

shout to say loudly and angrily

crowd a lot of people together

list a lot of names that you write one after the other

'What's on the list?'
Mulan asks Sun Ying.
'The **enemy** are now
here in our country,'
says Sun Ying,
'and we must **fight**
them. The **Emperor**
needs a very big **army**.'

'One man from every family must **join** the army tomorrow,' says Sun Ying.
'The names of all the men in the village are on the list.'

Mulan goes to the front of the crowd. She quickly reads the list.

enemy people who are not friends of your country

fight to hit someone again and again

emperor the most important man in a number of countries

army a large number of men who fight for their country

join to go with

4

'Oh, no!' cries Mulan. 'Look! My father's name is the first on the list.'

Hua Hu

Zhang Jie

'My father can't fight,' says Mulan. 'He's old and ill. And my brother, **Xiong**, is a young child. He can't join the army.'

'What can I do?' cries Mulan.

'You must think of a **plan**,' says Sun Ying.

Xiong /ʃʊŋ/

plan when you get something ready before it happens

READING CHECK

Match the first and second parts of the sentences.

a Mulan lives . . .
b Mulan's father is . . .
c Xiong is . . .
d At home Mulan is making . . .
e Mulan follows Sun Ying . . .
f A crowd of people is looking at . . .
g The Emperor needs . . .
h Mulan must think of . . .

1 a big army.
2 some cloth.
3 in a little village.
4 a plan.
5 young.
6 through the village.
7 old and ill.
8 a long list.

WORD WORK

1 Find nine more words from Chapter 1 in the wordsquare.

e	m	p	e	r	o	r	g	a	f
k	p	l	a	n	j	r	e	n	i
s	z	u	j	h	v	i	q	c	g
h	m	p	o	z	g	f	w	i	h
o	v	e	i	m	a	r	k	e	t
u	s	j	n	o	i	t	s	n	p
t	e	f	p	a	r	e	n	t	s
u	l	k	w	m	u	y	s	h	x
q	l	c	x	o	w	f	u	g	u
o	s	e	n	e	m	y	r	s	z

2 **Use the words from Activity 1 to complete the sentences.**

a The ..emperor. of China is an important man.

b Mulan lives with her . . . . , her older sister and her younger brother.

c Mulan makes cloth and . . . . it at the . . . . in the village.

d This is a very . . . . village. It's two thousand years old.

e The country needs a big army to . . . . the . . . .

f Mulan's brother can't . . . . the army because he's very young.

g 'What can we do tonight?' 'I have a . . . . We can go to a Chinese restaurant.'

h 'Don't . . . . ! I can hear you very well.'

GUESS WHAT

What happens in the next chapter? Tick one box.

a ☐ Mulan's father joins the army.

b ☐ Mulan's father doesn't join the army, and the emperor is angry with him.

c ☐ Mulan joins the army.

d ☐ Mulan and her family go away from their home village.

CHAPTER 2

Mulan runs home to her family. 'Mother, Father,' she cries. 'I have some bad **news**. The Emperor wants a man from every house to fight in the army.'

'Then I must go,' says her father. 'You can't go, you're ill,' says her mother.

'But when a man doesn't join the army the Emperor always **punishes** his family,' says her father.

'It's all right,' says Mulan. 'I'm young and **strong**. I can go **in Father's place**.'

'But how?' asks her mother. 'You're a girl and everybody knows it!'

news when someone tells you something that is new

punish to do something bad to someone after they do something bad

strong with a body that works well

in someone's place when you do something for someone because they can't do it

'I can be a man. I can learn to walk with my head up, and to shout when I talk,' she says. 'And I can wear **soldier's clothes**.'

'Mulan,' says her father, 'you're a **brave** daughter. You can join the army and **save** our family name.'

'Can I join the army with you?' asks Xiong.
Mulan laughs, 'You're a boy, Xiong. Perhaps you can be a soldier when you're a man.'

'Please be careful,' says her mother. Her father gives some money to her. 'You must be ready to join the army,' he says.

soldier a person in an army

clothes people wear these

brave not afraid

save to stop bad things happening to someone or something

Mulan needs to **buy** a horse. She runs to the market.

An old man calls to Mulan. 'Look at this horse,' he shouts. 'It's the best one in the village.' 'Can I **ride** it?' asks Mulan. 'Of course,' he says.

So Mulan gets on the horse and rides it. 'It's wonderful,' she says. 'How much is it?'

Later Mulan walks through the market with her new horse. She buys a beautiful **saddle** for it.

buy to give money for something

ride to go on a horse

saddle the thing that you put on a horse's back to sit on

When Mulan rides home from the market, she meets Sun Ying. 'Mulan!' shouts Sun Ying. 'You have a new horse! Where are you going?'

'It's a **secret**,' **whispers** Mulan. 'My plan is to join the army in my father's place.'
'You're very brave and **clever**, Mulan. But please be careful,' says Sun Ying. 'And good luck!'

The next day Mulan is ready to leave. 'Don't forget us,' whispers Xiong. He is crying. 'Please come home soon,' says her mother.

Mulan says goodbye to her family. She rides away quickly.

READING CHECK

Put these sentences in the correct order. Number them 1–8.

a ☐ Mulan goes to the market.

b ☐ Mulan tells her parents about her plan.

c ☐ Mulan rides away quickly.

d ☐ Mulan runs home.

e ☐ Mulan buys a horse.

f ☐ Mulan's family says goodbye to her.

g ☐ Mulan tells her secret to her friend Sun Ying.

h ☐ Mulan's father gives some money to her.

WORD WORK

1 Find words from Chapter 2 in the clothes.

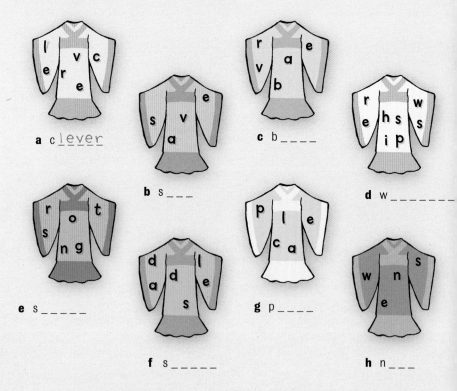

a c l̲e̲v̲e̲r̲

b s _ _ _

c b _ _ _ _ _

d w _ _ _ _ _ _ _ _

e s _ _ _ _ _ _

f s _ _ _ _ _ _

g p _ _ _ _ _

h n _ _ _ _

Complete the sentences with words from Activity 1.

a Mulan has a good plan; she's very c l e v e r .

b Mulan has some important _ _ _ _ about the names on the army list.

c Mulan joins the army in her father's _ _ _ _ _ _ .

d Mulan wants to join the army and _ _ _ _ the family name.

e Mulan isn't afraid to fight; she's very _ _ _ _ _ _ .

f Mulan _ _ _ _ _ _ _ _ her secret to Sun Ying.

g Mulan's horse has a new _ _ _ _ _ _ _ .

h Soldiers must walk far and fight well; they must be very _ _ _ _ _ _ _ .

GUESS WHAT

What does Mulan do in the next chapter? Tick the boxes.   **Yes**   **No**

Mulan . . .

a comes home after two weeks. The Emperor punishes her. ☐ ☐

b joins the army. Nobody knows she is a woman. ☐ ☐

c joins the army. She fights very bravely against the enemy. ☐ ☐

d leaves the army. Everybody laughs because she is a woman. ☐ ☐

e meets a friendly soldier – Ye Ming. He helps her. ☐ ☐

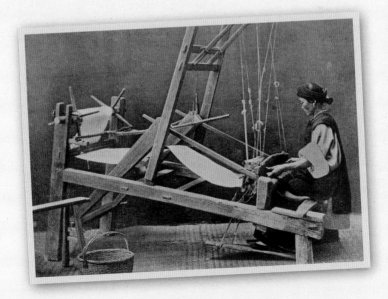

Mulan rides for two days . . .

. . . over the Black Hills . . .

. . . and across **rivers**.

She rides through the cold dark night, and through the **snow**. Then suddenly she sees hundreds of little **lights** in front of her.

She finds thousands of soldiers with their **tents** near the Yellow River. The light comes from their **fires**. She stops her horse and gets off.

river water that moves through the country in a long line

snow something soft, cold and white

light a thing that helps you to see in the dark

tent a house made of cloth that you can take with you when you move

fire this is red and hot, and it burns

'Hello there!' shouts one young man. 'Come and join us.'

'I'm Ye Ming,' he says. 'Would you like something hot to drink?'
'Yes, please. My name's Hua Mu—, sorry . . . Hua Hu,' says Mulan quickly.

'Come and sit by the fire,' shouts Ye Ming. 'This is Hua Hu,' he says to the soldiers near them.
'**Welcome** brother,' say the soldiers.

That night, Mulan sleeps in one of the tents.
'Everything is all right,' she thinks. 'I'm a woman but nobody knows my secret.'

welcome we say this when someone arrives and we are happy to see them

In the morning Ye Ming gets up early. 'Hua Hu,' he whispers. 'Are you **awake**?' 'We must get ready. The enemy is not far from us.'

All of the soldiers get ready for the **battle**. Then the **general** of the Chinese army talks to his men. 'Are you ready to fight?' he shouts. 'Yes!' they cry.

Later that morning the two armies meet.

The battle is long but Mulan fights bravely.

awake not sleeping

battle when two armies fight

general a very important person in an army

Hours later, many of the Chinese soldiers are dead. Mulan looks at them. 'Oh no, what can I do?' she thinks.

Suddenly she starts to ride **towards** the enemy. 'Brave soldiers follow me!' she cries.
The soldiers ride quickly after Mulan. She fights at the front with Ye Ming **next to** her.

An enemy soldier wants to kill Ye Ming. 'Watch out!' cries Mulan. Ye Ming rides away fast. 'Thank you!' he shouts to Mulan.

After many hours the Chinese army **wins** the battle.
The soldiers all come to Mulan. 'You're our **hero**!' they cry. 'We can win every battle now!'

owards nearer

ext to near

win to be the best in a battle

hero a person who does something brave or good

17

READING CHECK

Correct the mistakes.

two

a For ~~five~~ days Mulan rides across rivers and over hills.

b Mulan finds thousands of soldiers next to the Red River.

c Ye Ming gives Mulan a cold drink.

d The soldiers know Mulan's secret.

e The general of the Chinese army whispers to the soldiers.

f Mulan fights at the back of the army.

g An enemy soldier wants to kill Mulan.

h Ye Ming is now the hero of the army.

WORD WORK

1 Find words from Chapter 3 in the sword.

riversnowlightentfirewelcomeawakegeneraltowardswinnextto

2 **Use the words from Activity 1 to complete these sentences.**

a On holiday we don't stay in a hotel. We always sleep in a ....*tent*...... .

b It's very dark in here. We need a ....

c The Nile is a very long ....

d 'Do you feel cold? Come and sit near the ....'

e 'Is your young son ....?' 'No, he's asleep.'

f When someone arrives at your house, you can say '...............'.

g 'Where's the market?' 'Walk .... the supermarket and you can see it on the left.'

h His father is a very important person in the army; he's a ....

i It's very cold here in the winter and there's usually a lot of ....

j Mulan helps the Chinese army to .... the battle.

k Mulan always fights .... her friend Ye Ming.

GUESS WHAT

What happens in the next chapter? Tick the boxes.

a Mulan is now . . .

☐ the Emperor's friend.   ☐ a general.   ☐ with the enemy.

b When Mulan meets the Emperor, he . . .

☐ puts her in prison.   ☐ gives a house to her.   ☐ gives a horse to her.

Mulan fights in many more battles. Ye Ming always fights next to her.

'Hua Hu, you're very brave and clever!' say the soldiers. 'You must **lead** us into every battle.'

After some years Mulan **becomes** a general in the army. She **chases** the enemy out of China.

People all over the country hear of this **famous** soldier. But nobody knows her secret. Nobody knows her true name – Mulan!

lead to go in front

become to change from one thing to a different thing

chase to follow behind someone quickly

famous when many people know a person

One day a soldier visits Mulan. 'I have a **message** from the Emperor,' he says.

'What is it?' asks Mulan. 'You must come to the Emperor's **palace**,' says the soldier.

Mulan rides across the country with Ye Ming. Soon they arrive at the Emperor's palace.

message something that one person tells another person to say to someone

palace a big house where an emperor lives

'Hua Hu, your name is famous. You are the bravest soldier in China,' says the Emperor. 'Our country is **safe** now. I must thank you for that.'

Mulan **bows** in front of the Emperor. 'A soldier must live and fight for his country,' she says.

'What can I do for you?' the Emperor asks. 'Do you want to become a **minister**? Or would you like a big house?'

safe when something bad cannot happen there

bow to put down your head in front of someone or something important

minister an important person who helps an emperor

'No thank you,' says Mulan. 'But there is one thing . . .'

'What's that?' asks the Emperor. 'I want to go back to my family,' says Mulan. 'My father is an old man now and he needs my help.'

'Then leave the army and go home to your family,' says the Emperor. 'And please take my **finest** horse with you.'

'Oh, thank you, it's beautiful,' says Mulan.

fine beautiful

READING CHECK

Are these sentences true or false? Tick the boxes.

		True	False
a	Mulan becomes a general in the army.	☑	☐
b	The enemy leave China.	☐	☐
c	Everybody in China knows Mulan's secret.	☐	☐
d	The Emperor sends a message to Ye Ming.	☐	☐
e	Mulan and Ye Ming ride to the Emperor's palace.	☐	☐
f	The Emperor is angry with Mulan.	☐	☐
g	Mulan wants to go home to her family.	☐	☐
h	The Emperor gives Mulan a big house.	☐	☐

WORD WORK

Use the words in the horse to complete the sentences on page 25.

bow   message   minister   fine   palace   safe   famous   lead

a The Emperor lives in a very big .. *palace* . . .

b Mulan is a general. She must . . . . the army.

c Mulan chases the enemy out of China. The country is now . . . .

d A soldier gives Mulan a . . . . from the Emperor.

e When Mulan meets the Emperor, she must . . . . in front of him.

f Mulan doesn't want to work for the Emperor and become an important . . . .

g The Emperor is very happy with Mulan. He gives her a . . . . horse.

h The Great Wall of China is very . . . . Everybody knows about it.

GUESS WHAT

What happens in the next chapter? Read the sentences and write *Yes* or *No*.

a Mulan tells the Emperor, 'I am a woman.' The Emperor is very angry with her. . . . . . .

b Mulan says goodbye to Ye Ming. Then she rides home. . . . . .

c Mulan rides home. Ye Ming goes with her. . . . . .

d Mulan goes home but her father is dead. . . . . .

25

The next day Mulan is ready to leave the Emperor's palace.

Ye Ming comes to say goodbye.

'Hua Hu, thank you for saving my life,' he says. 'Please don't forget me.'

'How can I forget you?' says Mulan. 'You're my only true friend.'

Then Mulan begins the long **journey** home.

When she rides through villages, people come out of their houses and they **cheer**.

'Look! That's the famous general, Hua Hu,' they say excitedly. 'He's a true hero.'

ourney when you go far   **cheer** to shout happily

Soon her parents hear the news from a **traveller**. Mulan is coming home!

They make a big **feast**.

Mulan's brother, Xiong, is a young man now, and he puts **firecrackers** ready at the **gate**.

'When is Mulan coming home?' he asks every day.

traveller someone who goes on a journey

feast a lot of good things to eat

firecracker this makes a big noise when you put fire to it

gate a big door before the door of a house

The next morning Mulan arrives in the village.

Xiong runs out to see her. Mulan rides up to her house.

'Welcome home!' shouts Xiong over the noise of the firecrackers.

'Look at our daughter!' cries her mother. 'She is now an important general,' says her father. 'And she's riding the finest horse in the country!'

READING CHECK

Choose the correct pictures.

a Mulan says goodbye to . . .

b When Mulan rides through villages, people . . .

c Mulan's family make a . . . for Mulan.

d Every day . . . asks, 'When is Mulan coming home?'

e Mulan's brother puts . . . ready at the gate.

WORD WORK

Use the words in the lights to complete the sentences.

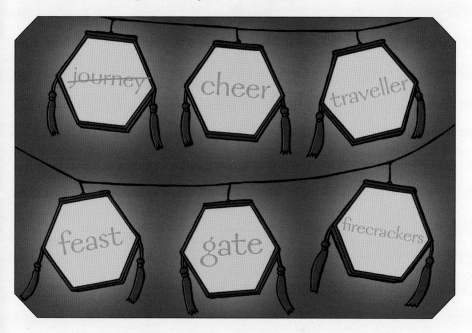

a Mulan has a very long . journey . ; she rides for days and days.

b When people see Mulan they . . . .

c Mulan's parents make a big . . . . for their daughter.

d Mulan is home! She is at the . . . . on her horse.

e That man is a . . . . He rides from village to village.

f Xiong welcomes Mulan home with . . . .

GUESS WHAT

What happens at the end of the story? Tick one box.

a ☐ Mulan joins the army again.

b ☐ Ye Ming sees Mulan in her women's clothes. He is angry and goes away.

c ☐ Ye Ming sees Mulan in her women's clothes. He loves her.

d ☐ The Emperor sees Mulan in her women's clothes. He punishes her.

31

'I'm a general now,' says Mulan and she smiles. 'But in an hour you can see your true daughter again.'

Mulan goes to her old room. First she takes off her soldier's clothes.

Next she puts on a fine dress, and **brushes** her long, dark hair.

brush to move something through your hair to make it look good

When Mulan comes out of her room she is beautiful. 'You're our daughter again!' cry her parents happily.

'Let's start the feast!' says her father. 'You must sit next to your father,' says her mother.

For hours and hours they talk and eat. Mulan tells them all about her **adventures** in the army. 'You're very brave!' says her friend, Sun Ying.

dventure something very exciting
nat happens to you

Mulan is happy to be at home again. Every day she helps her father.

One day she is making cloth in her room. Suddenly she hears a horse in the street. 'Hello there!' shouts a young man. 'Is there somebody at home?'

Mulan comes to the gate. The young man is Ye Ming. 'I'm looking for a young soldier. Hua Hu is his name . . .' he says, and then he stops.

'But it's you!' cries Ye Ming. 'You're Hua Hu, and you're a woman!' 'Yes, that's right!' says Mulan, and she laughs. 'Come in. I can **explain** everything.'

explain to talk to someone and make them understand something

Mulan and Ye Ming talk for a long time. They remember all their adventures, all their battles. 'It's good to talk to my best friend again,' says Ye Ming, and he smiles at Mulan.

Ye Ming meets Mulan's family. 'I'm very happy to meet you all,' he says. 'You have a very brave daughter.' 'Thank you,' says Mulan's father.

Ye Ming stays at the house for a week. Everybody in the family likes him.

One day, Ye Ming asks Mulan to **marry** him.
'I don't know,' answers Mulan. 'Can I marry my best friend from the army? We need to speak to my father.'

marry to make someone your husband or wife

Ye Ming goes to Mulan's father. 'Of course, you can marry my daughter,' he says and he smiles. 'Ask Mulan to come here.'

Mulan talks with her father for many hours that night.

The next day Ye Ming asks Mulan to marry him again. This time she says 'yes'. 'I'm truly happy,' she says to Ye Ming. 'Now you can be my best friend and my **husband**.'

husband the man that a woman marries

Mulan marries Ye Ming. Everybody in the village comes to the **wedding**.

Mulan and Ye Ming live happily in the village for many years.

And to this day, people talk about Hua Mulan, the bravest girl in China.

wedding the day when two people marry

READING CHECK

Choose the right words to finish the sentences.

a When Mulan goes to her room she puts on . . .
1 ☐ an old dress.
2 ☑ a fine dress.
3 ☐ soldier's clothes.

b At the feast Mulan tells everybody about her . . . in the army.
1 ☐ friends
2 ☐ enemies
3 ☐ adventures

c Mulan is . . . when Ye Ming arrives.
1 ☐ making a feast
2 ☐ making some cloth
3 ☐ helping her father

d Ye Ming stays with Mulan's family for . . .
1 ☐ one day.
2 ☐ a week.
3 ☐ a year.

e One day Ye Ming says to Mulan . . .
1 ☐ 'Come back to the army!'
2 ☐ 'Marry me!'
3 ☐ 'Goodbye!'

f In the end Mulan . . . Ye Ming.
1 ☐ marries
2 ☐ forgets
3 ☐ leaves

WORD WORK

1 Find words from Chapter 6 in the bowls.

a m _arry_

b e _ _ _ _ _ _

c w _ _ _ _ _ _

d h _ _ _ _ _ _

e b _ _ _ _

f a _ _ _ _ _ _ _ _ _

2 Use the words from Activity 1 to complete the sentences.

a Is it an interesting book?

Yes, it's about the adventures of a woman at sea.

b Can I take your photo?

Yes. But I want to . . . . my hair first.

c Hello, I'm Maria and this is my . . . . , Tony.

d Can you . . . . this word to me? I don't understand it.

Yes, of course.

e I love you! Please . . . . me!

No, sorry, I can't. I love your best friend!

f This is a picture of my sister's . . . .

I like her beautiful long dress.

Project A   *Things to see and do in Asia*

1 Look at the pictures and complete the poster.

Greetings from **CHINA**

the Great Wall of China

china vase

the Forbidden City

dumplings

mah-jong

the Yangtze River

In China . . .

a You can visit . . . . and . . . .
They are very famous places.

b You can go down . . . . on a boat.

c You can eat . . . . ; they're very good.

d People like playing . . . . ; it's a very interesting game!

e You can buy a beautiful . . . . to take home with you.

2 Look at these pictures of things to see and do in Japan. Write sentences about Japan.

In Japan . . .

3 Write about things to see and do in a different Asian country, or in your country.

Project B *A Story on a Plate*

1 Join the sentences with the words in brackets.

a Mulan makes cloth at home. Mulan sells it at the market. (and)

<u>Mulan makes cloth at home and she sells it at the market.</u>

b Mulan is a young woman. Mulan is strong and brave, too. (but)

....

c Mulan sees a list of names on a tree. Mulan reads it. (and)

....

d Xiong is very young. Xiong wants to join the army. (but)

....

e Mulan is a woman. Most people don't know that. (but)

....

f Mulan fights well. Mulan becomes a hero. (and)

....

2 Complete these sentences with *so* or *because*.

a China's enemy is coming nearer .... the emperor needs an army.

b Mulan's father is old and ill .... he can't fight in the army.

c Mulan becomes a soldier .... she's a brave young woman.

d The Emperor is happy with Mulan .... he gives a horse to her.

e Mulan's brother puts firecrackers ready .... he wants to welcome Mulan noisily when she comes home.

f Ye Ming marries Mulan .... he is in love with her.

3 Here is a story on a plate. Look at the pictures and read the story. Complete the sentences using *and*, *but*, *because*, or *so*.

A Mandarin – an important Chinese man – lives with his beautiful daughter, Koong-Se. A young man, Chang, works for the Mandarin. Koong-Se loves Chang (a) . . . . he has no money. Every day Koong-Se and Chang meet secretly under a tree in the garden.

One day Koong-Se's father hears about their secret. He chases Chang from the house (b) . . . . he is angry with him.

After that the Mandarin says to Koong-Se, 'Chang has no money (c) . . . . you can't marry him.' The Mandarin finds a new husband for Koong-Se (d) . . . . he asks hundreds of people to a big wedding feast.

Everybody drinks a lot at the feast (e) . . . . they sleep very well that night.

Later Chang secretly comes to the palace in a boat (f) . . . . he quietly takes Koong-Se away. They want to go to a small island (g) . . . . the Mandarin sees them. Quickly the Mandarin chases them over the river. In the end the two lovers become two lovebirds in the sky.

4 Complete these sentences to write the story of Mulan.

Mulan lives . . . .

Every day she. . . . .

But one day she sees. . . . .

Her father can't join the army because. . . . .

. . . .

So Mulan . . . .

Mulan fights bravely and. . . . .

After that the Emperor thanks Mulan and . . . .

. . . .

Mulan goes home but later . . . .

Now Ye Ming knows about Mulan's secret and. . . . .

. . . .

In the end Mulan . . . .

. . . .

GRAMMAR CHECK

Imperatives

Affirmative imperatives look the same as the infinitive without *to*.

Move! Look!

Negative imperatives start with do not or don't + infinitive without *to*.

Don't forget us.

We use imperatives to give instructions, orders, or invitations, or to make offers.

Be careful!   Brave soldiers follow me!   Come and join us!

Please take my finest horse with you.

Choose the correct word or words to complete the army rules.

a **Get up/~~Don't get up~~** late in the morning.

b **Leave/Don't leave** your clothes all over the tent.

c **Listen/Don't listen** carefully to the general.

d **Fight/Don't fight** bravely in all battles.

e **Run/Don't run** away from the enemy.

Mulan is leaving her family. Complete the sentences with the affirmative or negative imperative. Use the verbs in the box.

be	come	cry	~~forget~~	read	ride	tell	wear

a ' *Don't forget* your family,' says her father.

b '......... your horse carefully!' cries her mother.

c '......... people your true name,' whispers Sun Ying.

d '......... your soldier's clothes all the time,' says her father.

e '......... afraid!' shouts Sun Ying.

f '......... back soon and .... my books with me!' cries Xiong.

g 'Please .... , Xiong,' says Mulan. 'You can see me again soon.'

GRAMMAR CHECK

Modal auxiliary verbs: can and can't

We use can + infinitive without *to* to talk about things that we are able to do.

Mulan can fight bravely.   *Xiong can read.*

Can you lead the army into battle? Yes, I can.

We use can't + infinitive without *to* to describe things that we are not able to do.

Mulan's father can't fight because he's old and ill.

3 **Complete the sentences with *can* (✔) or *can't* (✗) and the verbs in brackets.**

a Mulan ..*can make*.. (✔ make) cloth but she ..*can't swim*.. (✗ swim) well.

b Mulan .... (✔ ride) quickly on her horse but she .... (✗ run) fast.

c Ye Ming .... (✗ write) quickly but he .... (✔ swim) well.

d Ye Ming .... (✔ paint) beautiful pictures but he .... (✗ make) cloth.

e Mulan .... (✔ cook) nice things to eat and she .... (✔ paint) wonderful pictures.

4 **Write questions for Mulan using words from parts A and B of the box.**

A	B
~~fight~~	a horse
ride	~~bravely~~
swim	soldiers into battle
lead	a fire
make	in a cold tent
sleep	across rivers

a *Can you fight bravely?* ....

b ....

c ....

d ....

e ....

f ....

GRAMMAR CHECK

Adverbs of frequency

We use adverbs of frequency to say how often something happens.

Ye Ming never forgets Mulan.   *Xiong sometimes asks his parents about Mulan.*

In Present Simple sentences, adverbs of frequency go in front of most verbs, but after the verb *be*.

Ye Ming always fights next to Mulan. The soldiers are always hungry.

always	usually	often	sometimes	never

Put the adverb of frequency in the correct place in the sentences.

a Children ⋏ have lots of exciting plans. (usually)
  usually

b Mulan's horse runs away. (never)

c Soldiers are afraid in a battle. (sometimes)

d Mulan makes cloth to sell at the market. (often)

e Chinese New Year is very important. (always)

Write the words in the correct order to make sentences.

a never / Mulan / true / says / name / her
   Mulan never says her true name.

b men / join / army / usually / the / Chinese
   ....

c often / is / father / ill / Mulan's
   ....

d soldiers / always / the / early / up / get
   ....

e thinks / sometimes / her / Mulan / friend / about
   ....

f Emperor / usually / is / happy / the / very
   ....

GRAMMAR

Countable and uncountable nouns

We can count countable nouns, and they can be singular or plural. We use a/an, the, or numbers in front of countable nouns.

a soldier	*the soldier*	*three soldiers*
an old man	*the old man*	*three old men*

We cannot count uncountable nouns, and they do not have a plural form. We use some in front of uncountable nouns.

Can you see some smoke?	*Would you like some lunch?*
Mulan's father needs some help.	*I've got some money.*

7 Complete the text with *a/an* or *some*.

One day, Mulan is doing a) ..some.. work at home. She is making b) .... cloth. Suddenly, she hears c) .... bad news. The Emperor needs d) .... soldier from every family for his big army. But Mulan's father is e) .... old man and he needs f) .... help when he walks.

So Mulan joins the army in her father's place. But first, she visits the market with g) .... money from her father. She buys h) .... horse and i) .... saddle. She gets j) .... bread, k) .... apple and many nice things to eat for her long ride, too.

The next morning, Mulan has l) .... breakfast and says goodbye to her family. She rides for two days and she suddenly sees m) .... smoke in the sky. She sees n) .... tent, too. Then she sees a lot more tents and   o) .... big fire. She is with the Chinese army now!

GRAMMAR CHECK

Possessive adjectives

We use possessive adjectives to show that something belongs to somebody, but we do not say who the person is.

This is <u>Mulan's</u> brother. → *This is her brother.*

That is <u>the soldier's</u> horse. → *That is his horse.*

Possessive adjectives go in front of the noun.

This is my saddle.   *Those are their tents.*

I → my	**he** → his	**she** → her	**it** → its
we → our	**you** → your	**they** → their	

Write the sentences again. Use possessive adjectives.

a This is <u>my feast and Ye Ming's</u> feast.

.....This is our feast......

b I know <u>Mulan's</u> secret.

....

c That is <u>the Emperor's</u> palace.

....

d The general is looking at <u>the horse's</u> foot.

....

e Here is <u>my parents'</u> house.

....

f Do you like <u>Sun Ying's</u> new dress? ....

Complete the sentences with the correct possessive adjectives.

a 'What's ...your... name?' 'I'm Sun Ying.'

b Please meet Ye Ming, my friend from the army. He's .... very best friend!

c 'Is your brother here?' 'Yes, he is. That is .... coat.'

d The dog always drinks .... water quickly.

e We live in a big house with .... three cats.

f At night, the soldiers all sleep in .... tents.

g Xiong has an older sister. .... name is Hua Mulan.

GRAMMAR CHECK

Articles: a/an, the

We use the indefinite article **a/an** when we talk about a singular noun, and it is not clear which of a number of things we may mean.

Mulan lives in a village.

We use **a** in front of a word that begins with a consonant sound and **an** in front of a word that begins with a vowel sound.

She is a general.   Her father is an old man.

We use the definite article **the** when we talk about singular and plural nouns, when it is clear which of several things we mean.

The next morning Mulan arrives in the village. (We know which one)

10 Complete the text with *a*, *an*, or *the*.

Dear Mulan

How are you? Do you think about us often? You're a) ....a.... soldier in b) .... Chinese army, I know, and perhaps you can't read this now. But I want to tell you some exciting news!

I've got c) .... new horse and I'm learning to ride! Father is teaching me. I've got d) .... fine, new saddle, too. e) .... horse is wonderful; it's f) .... best horse in g) .... village! I'm learning with h) .... friend — his name is Sheng Li. Do you know him? His father is i) .... teacher and they live in j) .... big, red house next to us.

Can you write me k) .... interesting letter soon? I want to hear all your news too!

Love,

Xiong

GRAMMAR CHECK

Phrasal verbs with get

A phrasal verb has two parts: a verb, such as get, and an adverb, such as on. Phrasal verbs with get usually talk about some kind of movement.

Mulan gets on her horse and rides it.

She stops her horse and gets off.

In the morning, Ye Ming and his friends get up early.

The soldiers quickly get out of the cold river.

Choose the correct word or words to complete the sentences.

a Don't forget to get **up/off** your horse when it is tired.

b We sometimes get **up/on** late in the morning.

c Don't get **on/off** the bed in your dirty shoes!

d Please help your father to get **out of/on** the car.

e I feel very safe when I get **on/up** my horse.

f You're standing on my foot! Please get **off/on**!

g Mulan usually gets **out of/up** bed early.

Complete the sentences with the correct form of the phrasal verbs in the box. You can use some of the verbs more than once.

get on	get off	get out of	get up

a Mulan .gets on. her horse and leaves the Emperor's palace.

b You must .... now! It's very late and your sister is coming home this morning.

c Ye Ming .... his horse and walks to the gate.

d The little girl can't see the general behind the crowd, so she .... a big chair.

e The soldiers .... the tent quickly and ride towards the enemy.

f Father always .... early and goes to bed early, too.

DOMINOES Your Choice

Read *Dominoes* for pleasure, or to develop language skills. It's your choice.

Each *Domino* reader includes:
- a good story to enjoy
- integrated activities to develop reading skills and increase vocabulary
- task-based projects – perfect for CEFR portfolios
- contextualized grammar activities

Each *Domino* pack contains a reader, and an excitingly dramatized audio recording of the story

If you liked this *Domino*, read these:

Sinbad
Retold by Janet Hardy-Gould
Sinbad the sailor spends many years at sea. He visits strange countries, meets some strange people and some very frightening animals. He is sometimes rich, sometimes poor . . . and always in danger. But all the time he is learning from his adventures, until finally he returns home to Baghdad, an older and wiser man.

The Big Story
John Escott
'Bring me something new and exciting. Bring me a BIG story!' says Rosie's editor at The Record newspaper.
And, when she leaves the office, Rosie does find a story. A story that is bigger than she expects. A story that takes her across Europe, into a dangerous world of art and art thieves.

	CEFR	Cambridge Exams	IELTS	TOEFL iBT	TOEIC
Level 3	B1	PET	4.0	57-86	550
Level 2	A2–B1	KET-PET	3.0-4.0	–	390
Level 1	A1–A2	YLE Flyers/KET	3.0	–	225
Starter & Quick Starter	A1	YLE Movers	1.0–2.0	–	–

You can find details and a full list of books and teachers' resources on our website:
www.oup.com/elt/gradedreaders